I0416569

THE SECRET OF PRICE INFLATION

"Unlocking Economic Stability in an Inflationary World"

VINCENT CLARK

Copyright ©

by Vincent Clark 2024 All rights reserved. This copy must first have permission from the publisher before being copied or otherwise replicated.

As a result, the information contained therein cannot be transferred, stored, or preserved in a database electronically. The document may not be copied, scanned, faxed, or retained in whole or part without the publisher's or author's consent.

Dedication

"To the curious minds and diligent seekers of economic wisdom, whose relentless pursuit of understanding fuels progress and prosperity. Your dedication to unraveling the complexities of price inflation inspires us all. In honor of those who strive to navigate the turbulent waters of economic instability with resilience and resolve, this book is dedicated. May its insights illuminate paths to stability and prosperity, guiding us through the ever-changing landscape of inflationary challenges. With heartfelt gratitude to those who dare to explore 'The Secret of Price Inflation' and the profound impact it holds on our world."

Table of Contents

Acknowledgment

"I extend my deepest appreciation to the economists, scholars, and researchers whose invaluable contributions have enriched the content of this book. Special thanks to my mentors for their guidance and expertise in shaping the narrative. I am grateful for the unwavering support of my family and friends, whose encouragement sustained me throughout this journey. I also acknowledge the countless individuals whose dedication to economic analysis and policymaking has paved the way for a deeper understanding of price inflation. This work stands as a testament to our collective pursuit of knowledge and our shared commitment to fostering economic stability."

Preface

In an era marked by economic uncertainty and volatility, the phenomenon of price inflation remains a perplexing enigma, affecting individuals, businesses, and nations worldwide. "The Secret of Price Inflation" embarks on a journey to unravel this complex and often misunderstood aspect of modern economics.

In this book, we embark on a journey to explore the intricate mechanisms underlying price inflation, shedding light on its origins, impacts, and potential remedies. Drawing upon decades of economic research, real-world examples, and insightful analysis, this book seeks to demystify the forces driving inflationary pressures in our global economy. From the fundamental principles of supply and demand to the intricate interplay of monetary and fiscal policies, each chapter delves deeper into the labyrinth of inflationary dynamics. Along the way, we examine the role of consumer behavior, technological advancements, and globalization in shaping price trends, offering readers a comprehensive understanding of the multifaceted nature of inflation.

As we navigate through these pages, I invite you to embark on a journey of discovery, to challenge preconceived notions, and to engage with the complexities of price inflation with curiosity and an open mind. Together, let us uncover "The Secret of Price Inflation" and empower ourselves to navigate the economic landscape with clarity and confidence.

Chapter 1:

Unraveling the Mysteries of Inflation

- Understanding the Basics: What Is Inflation?

Inflation, an economic phenomenon often discussed in financial circles, refers to the sustained increase in the general price level of goods and services within an economy over some time. It is essentially a decrease in the purchasing power of money, as more units of currency are required to purchase the same quantity of goods or services. While inflation is a common occurrence in modern economies, its causes, effects, and management strategies can be complex and multifaceted.

One of the primary drivers of inflation is excess demand relative to supply. When demand for goods and services outpaces their availability, prices tend to rise as consumers compete for limited resources. This demand-pull inflation is often associated with periods of economic growth, increased consumer spending, or expansionary monetary policies.

Another significant cause of inflation is cost-push inflation, which occurs when production costs, such as wages or raw materials, increase, leading producers to pass these higher costs onto consumers through higher prices. This type of inflation can be triggered by factors like rising energy prices, supply chain disruptions, or government regulations.

Expectations also play a crucial role in shaping inflation dynamics. If individuals and businesses anticipate future price increases, they may adjust their behavior accordingly, leading to self-fulfilling prophecies of inflationary pressure. Central banks and policymakers closely monitor inflation expectations and often employ monetary policy tools, such as interest rate adjustments or open market operations, to manage inflation and stabilize prices.

Understanding the basics of inflation is essential for individuals, businesses, and policymakers alike, as it impacts various aspects of the economy, including savings, investments, wages, and overall economic stability. By unraveling the mysteries of inflation and grasping its underlying mechanisms, stakeholders can make more informed decisions to navigate the complex economic landscape effectively.

- Historical Perspectives: Tracing the Origins of Inflation

Tracing the origins of inflation reveals a fascinating journey through economic history, with its roots extending back to ancient civilizations. While modern understanding of inflation primarily focuses on monetary and fiscal policies, historical perspectives shed light on diverse factors contributing to inflationary episodes throughout time.

One of the earliest recorded instances of inflation dates back to the Roman Empire, where debasement of currency, and reducing the precious metal content of coins, was a common practice to finance military campaigns and cover fiscal deficits. This manipulation of currency supply led to a decline in purchasing power, contributing to economic instability and social unrest.

In medieval Europe, the influx of gold and silver from the New World fueled inflation as increased bullion circulation outpaced the growth of goods and services in the economy. This period, known as the Price Revolution, saw a significant rise in prices, altering consumption patterns and redistributing wealth within society.

During the Industrial Revolution, technological advancements and increased productivity drove economic growth but also introduced new inflationary pressures. Rapid urbanization, coupled with expanding markets and rising wages, fueled demand for goods and services, resulting in inflationary spikes in certain sectors.

In the 20th century, the aftermath of World Wars and the Great Depression saw governments resorting to expansionary fiscal and monetary policies to stimulate economic recovery. However, these policies often led to inflationary spirals, as increased government spending and loose monetary conditions outpaced productive capacity, triggering inflation.

In more recent times, globalization and financialization have reshaped the dynamics of inflation, with interconnected economies and financial markets amplifying the transmission of inflationary pressures across borders.

Understanding the historical origins of inflation underscores its complex interplay of economic, political, and social factors. By examining past inflationary episodes, policymakers gain valuable insights into designing effective strategies to mitigate inflationary risks and maintain macroeconomic stability in the modern era.

- The Impact on Economies and Individuals

The impact of inflation on economies and individuals is profound and multifaceted, influencing various aspects of economic activity and everyday life. At the macroeconomic level, persistent inflation can erode purchasing power, disrupt price stability, and hinder long-term economic growth.

One of the primary effects of inflation is the reduction in the real value of money. As prices rise, each unit of currency buys fewer goods and services, diminishing the standard of living for individuals and households. This erosion of purchasing power can particularly affect fixed-income earners, retirees, and those with limited financial assets, leading to a decline in their real incomes and living standards.

Inflation also distorts economic decision-making and resource allocation. Uncertainty about future prices can undermine investment incentives, as businesses may delay capital expenditures or hold excess cash to hedge against inflationary risks. This reluctance to invest can dampen productivity growth and hinder overall economic expansion.

Moreover, inflation can exacerbate wealth inequality within society. Those with assets that appreciate during inflationary periods, such as real estate or stocks, may see their wealth grow, widening the gap between the rich and the poor. Meanwhile, individuals with fixed incomes or savings in cash or low-yielding assets bear the brunt of inflation's negative effects, exacerbating income disparities.

At the national level, inflation can undermine a country's competitiveness in global markets. Rising domestic prices may reduce export competitiveness, leading to a deterioration in the trade balance and potential currency depreciation. Additionally, inflationary pressures can prompt central banks to tighten monetary policy, raising interest rates to curb inflation but potentially slowing down economic activity and increasing borrowing costs for businesses and consumers.

Overall, the impact of inflation on economies and individuals underscores the importance of maintaining price stability and implementing sound monetary and fiscal policies to mitigate inflationary risks and promote sustainable economic growth and prosperity.

Chapter 2:

The Invisible Forces at Play

- Supply and Demand Dynamics

Supply and demand dynamics are fundamental invisible forces that play a pivotal role in shaping inflationary pressures within an economy. Understanding these dynamics illuminates how shifts in supply and demand for goods and services influence price levels and ultimately contribute to inflationary or deflationary conditions.

On the supply side, changes in production capacity, input costs, and technology can influence the availability of goods and services. When supply struggles to keep pace with growing demand, shortages can occur, driving prices upward as consumers compete for limited resources. Conversely, increased production efficiency or expanded capacity can alleviate supply constraints, exerting downward pressure on prices.

Demand dynamics, on the other hand, are driven by factors such as consumer preferences, income levels, and economic expectations. Strong consumer demand fueled by rising incomes or optimistic economic outlooks can lead to increased spending, driving prices higher through demand-pull inflation. Conversely, subdued demand stemming from economic downturns or consumer pessimism can lead to deflationary pressures as businesses lower prices to stimulate sales.

Supply and demand imbalances can manifest across different sectors of the economy, contributing to sector-specific inflationary pressures. For example, disruptions in the supply chain, such as natural disasters or geopolitical events, can lead to shortages of essential commodities, causing prices to spike. Similarly, shifts in consumer preferences towards certain products or services can create localized demand surges, driving up prices within specific markets.

Central banks and policymakers closely monitor supply and demand dynamics to gauge inflationary risks and formulate appropriate monetary policies. By influencing interest rates, money supply, and economic incentives, policymakers aim to stabilize inflation at levels conducive to sustainable economic growth and price stability.

Understanding the intricate interplay between supply and demand dynamics provides valuable insights into the underlying drivers of inflationary pressures within an economy. By addressing supply constraints, stimulating demand, and implementing effective policy measures, stakeholders can navigate the invisible forces at play and promote macroeconomic stability in the face of inflationary challenges.

- Monetary Policy: The Role of Central Banks

Central banks play a crucial role in influencing inflation through monetary policy. Their primary mandate often includes maintaining price stability, which involves keeping inflation within a target range conducive to sustainable economic growth. Central banks employ various tools to achieve this objective, with monetary policy being one of the most powerful instruments at their disposal.

Monetary policy refers to the actions undertaken by central banks to regulate the money supply, interest rates, and credit conditions in the economy. By adjusting these variables, central banks aim to influence aggregate demand, inflation expectations, and overall economic activity.

One of the key mechanisms through which central banks influence inflation is by setting short-term interest rates, such as the federal funds rate in the United States or the policy rate in other countries. By raising or lowering interest rates, central banks can affect borrowing costs for businesses and consumers, thereby influencing spending and investment decisions. For example, during periods of high inflation, central banks may raise interest rates to curb excessive borrowing and spending, dampening inflationary pressures. Conversely, during economic downturns or periods of low inflation, central banks may lower interest rates to stimulate borrowing and spending, thereby boosting economic activity and inflation.

In addition to setting interest rates, central banks also engage in open market operations, which involve buying or selling government securities in the open market. By purchasing government securities, central banks inject liquidity into the banking system, lowering interest rates and stimulating lending and spending. Conversely, by selling government securities, central banks can drain liquidity from the banking system, raising interest rates and curbing inflationary pressures.

Furthermore, central banks may use unconventional monetary policy tools, such as quantitative easing (QE), to further influence inflation. QE involves the large-scale purchase of financial assets, such as government bonds or mortgage-backed securities, to lower long-term interest rates and stimulate lending and investment.

Overall, central banks play a pivotal role in shaping inflation through their control over monetary policy. By adjusting interest rates, conducting open market operations, and employing unconventional policy tools, central banks aim to achieve their inflation targets and promote macroeconomic stability.

- Fiscal Policy: Government Intervention and Its Effects

Fiscal policy, controlled by governments, complements monetary policy in influencing inflation and overall economic activity. Unlike monetary policy, which is primarily executed by central banks, fiscal policy involves government decisions regarding taxation, spending, and borrowing.

During periods of high inflation, governments may implement contractionary fiscal policies to curb excess demand and stabilize prices. This can involve reducing government spending, raising taxes, or a combination of both. By reducing aggregate demand, contractionary fiscal policies aim to dampen inflationary pressures and prevent overheating in the economy.

Conversely, during economic downturns or periods of low inflation, governments may implement expansionary fiscal policies to stimulate demand and support economic growth. This can involve increasing government spending on infrastructure projects, social programs, or tax cuts to boost consumer and business spending. By increasing aggregate demand, expansionary fiscal policies aim to mitigate deflationary risks and stimulate economic activity.

However, the effectiveness of fiscal policy in influencing inflation depends on various factors, including the timing, magnitude, and composition of fiscal measures, as well as the overall economic environment.

For example, if implemented too aggressively or during a period of full employment, expansionary fiscal policies can exacerbate inflationary pressures and lead to overheating in the economy. Similarly, contractionary fiscal policies implemented during an economic downturn can worsen deflationary pressures and prolong the recession.

Moreover, the effectiveness of fiscal policy in influencing inflation can be constrained by factors such as fiscal sustainability, political considerations, and the presence of structural rigidities in the economy. In some cases, governments may face challenges in implementing fiscal measures due to political gridlock, budgetary constraints, or limited fiscal space.

Overall, while fiscal policy can play a significant role in influencing inflation and economic activity, its effectiveness depends on various factors and must be carefully calibrated to achieve desired outcomes. By working in tandem with monetary policy and other policy tools, fiscal authorities can help maintain price stability and promote sustainable economic growth.

Chapter 3:

Unveiling the Secrets of Price Determinants

- Factors Influencing Price Inflation

Price inflation is influenced by a complex interplay of factors that encompass both demand and supply dynamics within an economy. Understanding these determinants is essential for unraveling the secrets of price inflation and its impact on various economic agents.

1. Consumer Demand: Demand-pull inflation occurs when consumer demand exceeds the available supply of goods and services. Factors such as rising incomes,

consumer confidence, and changes in preferences can drive increased demand, putting upward pressure on prices.

2. Cost of Production: Cost-push inflation occurs when production costs, such as wages, raw materials, and energy prices, rise, causing firms to pass on these higher costs to consumers through increased prices. Supply chain disruptions, changes in labor market conditions, and government regulations can contribute to cost-push inflation.

3. Monetary Factors: Changes in the money supply, interest rates, and exchange rates can influence inflationary pressures. Expansionary monetary policies, such as lowering interest rates or increasing the money supply, can stimulate spending and investment, potentially leading to

inflation. Similarly, currency depreciation can increase the cost of imported goods, contributing to inflation.

4. Supply Constraints: Supply shortages or disruptions, whether due to natural disasters, geopolitical events, or trade restrictions, can limit the availability of goods and services, driving prices higher. Supply chain bottlenecks, capacity constraints, and technological disruptions can also contribute to supply-side inflationary pressures.

5. Inflation Expectations: Expectations about future price movements can influence current inflation dynamics. If businesses and consumers anticipate higher prices in the future, they may adjust their behavior accordingly, leading to self-fulfilling prophecies of inflation.

6. Government Policies: Fiscal and regulatory policies can have significant implications for inflation. Government spending programs, taxation policies, subsidies, and regulations can affect aggregate demand and supply conditions, influencing inflationary pressures.

7. Global Factors: Economic developments and events in the global economy can impact domestic inflation. Changes in global commodity prices, exchange rates, and trade patterns can transmit inflationary pressures across borders.

By considering these factors influencing price inflation, policymakers, businesses, and individuals can better anticipate and respond to inflationary trends, ensuring sound economic decision-making and promoting price stability in the long run.

- Globalization and Its Impact on Prices

Globalization has profoundly influenced price dynamics, introducing both opportunities and challenges for economies around the world. Its impact on prices is multifaceted, affecting various sectors and contributing to both inflationary and deflationary pressures.

1. Imported Goods: Globalization has facilitated the movement of goods and services across borders, allowing consumers access to a wide range of

products from around the world. As a result, increased competition from imports can lead to lower prices for imported goods, benefiting consumers and exerting downward pressure on domestic prices.

2. **Outsourcing and Offshoring:** Companies often seek lower production costs by outsourcing manufacturing or services to countries with lower labor costs. While this can result in cheaper goods for consumers, it may also lead to job losses and downward pressure on wages in higher-cost countries.

3. Global Supply Chains: The integration of global supply chains has made economies more interconnected and susceptible to disruptions. Supply chain disruptions, such as natural disasters or geopolitical tensions, can lead to shortages

of critical components or raw materials, driving prices higher.

4. Exchange Rates: Globalization has increased the importance of exchange rates in determining the prices of imported and exported goods. Currency fluctuations can affect the cost of imports and exports, influencing domestic price levels. A depreciating domestic currency can increase the cost of imported goods, contributing to inflationary pressures.

5. Commodity Prices: Globalization has led to increased trade in commodities such as oil, metals, and agricultural products. Changes in global commodity prices can have significant implications for domestic inflation. Rising commodity prices can increase production costs and input prices

for businesses, leading to higher consumer prices.

6. Global Economic Conditions: Economic developments in major economies can impact global demand and supply conditions, affecting prices worldwide. For example, a slowdown in global economic growth can lead to weaker demand for commodities, putting downward pressure on prices.

7. Supply and Demand Imbalances: Globalization has led to disparities in supply and demand conditions across different regions. Demand surges or supply shortages in one part of the world can spill over into other regions, affecting prices globally.

Overall, globalization has reshaped price dynamics, introducing greater interconnectedness and complexity into the global economy. While it has contributed to lower prices for some goods and services, it has also brought about challenges such as supply chain vulnerabilities and increased exposure to external shocks. Understanding the impact of globalization on prices is essential for policymakers and businesses to navigate the complexities of the modern global economy.

- Technological Advancements and Price Dynamics

Technological advancements have profoundly influenced price dynamics, shaping consumer behavior, production processes, and market structures. The impact of technology on prices is multifaceted, with both inflationary and deflationary effects across various sectors.

1. Increased Efficiency: Technological innovations often lead to increased productivity and efficiency in production processes. Automation, robotics, and advanced manufacturing techniques allow firms to produce more goods and services at lower costs, leading to downward pressure on prices.

2. Price Transparency: The proliferation of e-commerce platforms and price comparison websites has increased price transparency, allowing consumers to easily compare prices across different retailers. This heightened transparency fosters greater competition, incentivizing firms to lower prices to attract customers.

3. Disruptive Technologies: Disruptive technologies, such as blockchain, artificial intelligence, and 3D printing, have the potential to revolutionize industries and disrupt traditional business models. These innovations can lead to cost reductions, product customization, and new market entrants, all of which can impact price dynamics.

4. Productivity Growth: Technological advancements drive long-term

productivity growth, which can have deflationary effects on prices. As economies become more productive, the cost of producing goods and services decreases, leading to lower prices for consumers.

5. Demand Creation: Technology often creates new products and services, stimulating consumer demand and potentially leading to price increases in those segments. For example, the introduction of smartphones and other electronic devices has created new markets and driven up prices in the technology sector.

6. Network Effects: Technological platforms and networks, such as social media and online marketplaces, can benefit from network effects, where the

value of the platform increases as more users join. This can lead to pricing power for platform owners, potentially resulting in higher prices for users.

7.   Environmental   Considerations: Technological   innovations   aimed   at addressing environmental challenges, such as renewable energy technologies and energy-efficient appliances, can impact prices by altering production costs and consumer preferences.

Overall, technological advancements have a profound impact on price dynamics, influencing both the cost side and demand side of the economy. While technology has the potential to drive down prices through   increased   efficiency   and competition, it can also create new markets and demand drivers that lead to price increases in certain segments. Understanding the interplay between technology and prices is essential for businesses and policymakers to anticipate and respond to changes in the marketplace.

Chapter 4:

The Psychology of Pricing

- Consumer Behavior and Perception

The psychology of pricing is a fascinating field that explores how consumers perceive and react to various pricing strategies. Consumer behavior and perception play crucial roles in shaping purchasing decisions, and businesses often leverage psychological principles to influence these decisions.

One fundamental concept in pricing psychology is price anchoring. This occurs when consumers rely heavily on the first price they encounter as a reference point for judging subsequent prices. For example, a high initial price can make subsequent, slightly lower prices seem more reasonable or even like a bargain. Businesses strategically use price anchoring to shape consumers' perceptions of value and willingness to pay.

Decoy pricing is another tactic based on consumer psychology. It involves presenting a third option, known as a decoy, alongside two main options to influence consumers to choose a particular option. The decoy is priced in a way that makes one of the main options appear more attractive, even if it's not the most cost-effective choice. This strategy exploits consumers' tendency to compare options relative to each other rather than assessing absolute value.

Furthermore, the framing effect highlights how the presentation of information can significantly impact consumer perceptions. By framing prices in a certain context, such as emphasizing savings or highlighting premium features, businesses can influence how consumers evaluate the value proposition of a product or service.

Additionally, consumers often perceive pricing cues beyond the numerical value, such as price endings (e.g., $9.99 vs. $10.00) or the use of prestige pricing (setting higher prices to convey luxury or quality). These subtle cues can evoke different emotional responses and influence purchasing decisions.

In conclusion, understanding the psychology of pricing is essential for businesses to effectively position their products or services in the marketplace. By leveraging consumer behavior and perception, businesses can optimize pricing strategies to enhance perceived value, increase sales, and ultimately drive profitability.

- Behavioral Economics Insights

Behavioral economics, a field blending psychology and economics, offers profound insights into how people make decisions, revealing that individuals often behave in ways that defy traditional economic theory. By understanding these insights, businesses, and policymakers can design more effective strategies and policies that account for real-world human behavior.

One key insight from behavioral economics is the concept of bounded rationality, proposed by Nobel laureate Herbert Simon. Bounded rationality suggests that individuals do not always make fully rational decisions due to cognitive limitations, information overload, and time constraints. Instead, people often rely on heuristics—mental shortcuts or rules of thumb—to simplify decision-making processes. Businesses can leverage this understanding by designing products and services that align with consumers' cognitive biases and heuristics.

Another important concept is loss aversion, first articulated by Daniel Kahneman and Amos Tversky. Loss aversion refers to the tendency for individuals to strongly prefer avoiding losses over acquiring equivalent gains. This asymmetry in decision-making can lead to risk aversion and status quo bias, where people are reluctant to change from their current state, even if a change could lead to better outcomes. Businesses can mitigate loss aversion by framing choices in terms of potential gains rather than losses, or by offering risk-free trials to overcome inertia.

Furthermore, behavioral economics highlights the power of social norms and context in shaping behavior. People are influenced by the behavior of others and are more likely to conform to social norms. This insight can be harnessed by businesses through techniques such as social proof and peer influence, where testimonials, user reviews, or endorsements are used to persuade consumers.

However, behavioral economics provides valuable insights into human decision-making processes, revealing the complexities and biases that influence behavior. By incorporating these insights into their strategies and policies, businesses and policymakers can better understand and anticipate how individuals will respond to choices and interventions, ultimately leading to more effective outcomes.

- Marketing Strategies and Price Perception

Marketing strategies can significantly influence price perception among consumers. By understanding how consumers perceive prices, businesses can implement effective marketing strategies to convey value and drive sales.

One key aspect of price perception is the perceived value of a product or service. Marketing strategies such as highlighting product features, emphasizing quality, or showcasing unique selling points can enhance perceived value, making consumers more willing to pay a higher price. Additionally, using persuasive language or imagery in marketing materials can create a perception of exclusivity or luxury, further influencing consumers' willingness to pay.

Another important factor is price comparison. Consumers often rely on comparisons with similar products or services to assess whether a price is fair or competitive. Marketing strategies that position a product as superior to competitors or emphasize its unique benefits can justify a higher price in the minds of consumers. Additionally, offering price comparisons with higher-priced alternatives or highlighting discounts and promotions can create a perception of value and affordability.

Furthermore, the way prices are presented can impact perception. Strategies such as using charm pricing (e.g., pricing products at $9.99 instead of $10) or bundling products together can make prices appear more appealing to consumers. Similarly, framing prices in terms of savings or emphasizing the value proposition can influence consumers' perceptions of price fairness and attractiveness.

Moreover, branding and reputation play a crucial role in price perception. Strong brands often command higher prices due to the perceived quality, reliability, and prestige associated with the brand. Marketing strategies that build brand equity through consistent messaging, positive associations, and memorable experiences can support higher price points and foster consumer trust and loyalty.

In essence, marketing strategies play a vital role in shaping price perception among consumers. By effectively communicating value, highlighting competitive advantages, and leveraging psychological pricing tactics, businesses can influence how consumers perceive prices and ultimately drive purchase behavior.

Chapter 5:

Navigating the Complexities of Inflation Measurement

- CPI vs. PPI: Understanding the Differences

In navigating the complexities of inflation measurement, understanding the differences between the Consumer Price Index (CPI) and the Producer Price Index (PPI) is essential. While both indices measure price changes over time, they serve different purposes and focus on distinct segments of the economy.

The Consumer Price Index (CPI) tracks the changes in prices paid by urban consumers for a basket of goods and services over time. It reflects the average price level experienced by households and is widely used to assess changes in the cost of living. CPI includes a broad range of consumer expenditures, such as food, housing, transportation, and healthcare. It is crucial for policymakers in making decisions related to fiscal and monetary policies, as well as for individuals in adjusting wages, benefits, and investment strategies.

On the other hand, the Producer Price Index (PPI) measures the average change in selling prices received by domestic producers of goods and services over time. Unlike the CPI, which focuses on consumer purchases, the PPI captures price changes at the wholesale or producer level. It includes prices received for goods, services, and construction sold by domestic producers and is often used as an indicator of inflationary pressures within the production process. The PPI provides insights into input costs for businesses, which can influence pricing decisions, profit margins, and investment strategies.

While both indices are essential for understanding inflation dynamics, they have different methodologies, coverage, and implications. CPI typically includes a broader range of goods and services relevant to consumers, while PPI focuses more on intermediate and finished goods at the producer level. Additionally, CPI may incorporate measures such as housing costs and taxes, which are not included in PPI calculations.

In summary, understanding the distinctions between CPI and PPI is crucial for policymakers, economists, businesses, and consumers in accurately assessing inflationary trends, making informed decisions, and mitigating economic risks. By considering the unique perspectives offered by each index, stakeholders can gain a more comprehensive understanding of inflation dynamics and their implications for the economy.

- Critiques of Inflation Indices

Critiques of inflation indices, such as the Consumer Price Index (CPI) and the Producer Price Index (PPI), highlight various limitations and challenges in accurately measuring changes in the cost of living and production over time. Some of the key critiques include:

1. Composition Bias: One common critique is composition bias, which arises when changes in the quality or quantity of goods and services are not adequately accounted for in the index. For example, if the price of a product increases but its quality also improves, the index may overstate the true increase in the cost of living. Similarly, shifts in consumer preferences or the availability of substitute goods may not be reflected accurately in the index.

2. Substitution Bias: Substitution bias occurs when consumers respond to price changes by substituting cheaper alternatives for more expensive ones. While CPI attempts to account for this

through a concept called "hedonic pricing" and the use of substitution patterns, some argue that these adjustments may not fully capture real-world consumer behavior, leading to an overestimation or underestimation of inflation.

3. Geometric Mean Formula: The geometric mean formula used in inflation indices, particularly in CPI calculations, has been criticized for its potential to underestimate inflation. Critics argue that the formula may not adequately reflect the way consumers allocate their spending across different categories, leading to distortions in the index.

4. Treatment of Housing Costs: Housing costs, including rent and homeownership expenses, pose challenges in inflation measurement. CPI typically uses measures

such as owners' equivalent rent to estimate housing costs, which may not accurately reflect changes in housing prices. Additionally, fluctuations in housing markets can introduce volatility and measurement errors into the index.

5. Exclusion of Asset Prices: Traditional inflation indices such as CPI and PPI focus on goods and services consumed by households or produced by businesses. However, they do not include changes in asset prices such as stocks, bonds, or real estate, which can also have significant implications for individuals' wealth and financial well-being.

Addressing these critiques requires ongoing refinement of inflation measurement methodologies, including the development of more accurate price indices, improvements in data collection techniques, and increased transparency in index calculations. Despite these challenges, inflation indices remain valuable tools for policymakers, economists, businesses, and consumers in understanding and responding to changes in the economy.

- Alternative Measures and Their Significance

Alternative measures of inflation provide additional perspectives on changes in prices and cost of living, complementing traditional indices such as the Consumer Price Index (CPI) and the Producer Price Index (PPI). These alternative measures offer insights into specific aspects of inflation dynamics and can help address some of the critiques leveled against traditional indices. Some significant alternative measures include:

1. Core Inflation: Core inflation excludes volatile components such as food and energy prices from the index, focusing on underlying inflation trends. By removing these volatile elements, core inflation aims to provide a more stable measure of inflationary pressures. Core inflation is often used by policymakers and economists to gauge long-term inflation trends and guide monetary policy decisions.

2. Trimmed Mean Inflation: Trimmed mean inflation calculates inflation based on the average price change after excluding a certain percentage of the most

extreme price movements. This approach aims to mitigate the impact of outliers and temporary fluctuations in prices, providing a smoother and more robust measure of underlying inflationary trends.

3. Personal Consumption Expenditures (PCE) Price Index: The PCE price index, published by the U.S. Bureau of Economic Analysis, measures changes in prices of goods and services purchased by households. Unlike CPI, which uses a fixed basket of goods, PCE adjusts for changes in consumer behavior and spending patterns over time. It also incorporates data from a wider range of sources, providing a more comprehensive picture of inflationary pressures.

4. Medical Care Inflation: Medical care inflation focuses specifically on changes

in healthcare costs, including medical services, prescription drugs, and health insurance premiums. Given the significant impact of healthcare expenses on household budgets, tracking medical care inflation is crucial for understanding overall cost-of-living increases and assessing the affordability of healthcare services.

5. Asset Price Inflation: Asset price inflation measures changes in the prices of financial assets such as stocks, bonds, and real estate. While not traditionally included in inflation indices like CPI or PPI, asset price inflation is important for assessing wealth effects, financial stability, and the distributional impact of monetary policy.

These alternative measures of inflation provide valuable insights into specific components of the economy and can help policymakers, economists, businesses, and consumers make more informed decisions. By considering a range of inflation measures, stakeholders can gain a deeper understanding of inflation dynamics and better navigate economic challenges and opportunities.

Chapter 6:

Strategies for Mitigating the Effects of Inflation

- Investment Strategies for Inflationary Environments

Inflation erodes the purchasing power of money over time, making it crucial for investors to employ strategies that mitigate its effects and preserve wealth during inflationary periods. Here are some investment strategies tailored for inflationary environments:

1. Stocks with Pricing Power: Invest in companies with strong pricing power, meaning they can raise prices in line with inflation without losing customers. These

companies often operate in sectors such as consumer staples, utilities, and healthcare, where demand for their products remains relatively stable regardless of economic conditions.

2. Real Assets: Allocate a portion of your portfolio to real assets such as real estate, commodities, and infrastructure. Real assets have intrinsic value and tend to appreciate during inflationary periods, providing a hedge against inflation. Consider investments in real estate investment trusts (REITs), precious metals like gold and silver, and energy commodities like oil and natural gas.

3. Inflation-Linked Bonds: Invest in inflation-linked bonds, also known as Treasury Inflation-Protected Securities (TIPS) in the United States. These bonds

adjust their principal and interest payments based on changes in the consumer price index (CPI), providing investors with protection against inflation. TIPS offers a guaranteed real return above inflation, making them attractive during inflationary environments.

4. Commodities and Natural Resources: Diversify your portfolio with investments in commodities and natural resource companies. Commodities such as agricultural products, metals, and energy tend to appreciate during inflationary periods due to increased demand and higher production costs. Consider investing in commodity index funds, commodity futures, or shares of companies engaged in resource extraction and production.

5. Dividend-Paying Stocks: Invest in dividend-paying stocks, particularly those with a track record of consistently increasing dividends over time. Dividend income provides a reliable source of cash flow that can help offset the effects of inflation. Look for companies with stable earnings, strong cash flow generation, and a history of dividend growth, especially in sectors less susceptible to economic downturns.

6. Global Diversification: Diversify your investment portfolio globally to access opportunities in different regions and benefit from currency diversification. Investing in assets denominated in foreign currencies can provide additional protection against domestic inflationary pressures and currency depreciation.

7. Short-Term Investments: Consider allocating a portion of your portfolio to short-term investments with liquidity and flexibility. Short-term investments such as Treasury bills, money market funds, and short-duration bonds provide capital preservation and can be rolled over at higher interest rates as inflation rises.

By implementing these investment strategies, investors can effectively mitigate the effects of inflation and preserve the purchasing power of their wealth over the long term. However, it's essential to carefully assess individual risk tolerance, investment objectives, and time horizons before making investment decisions. Consulting with a financial advisor can provide personalized guidance tailored to your specific financial situation and goals.

- Hedging Techniques and Risk Management

Hedging techniques and risk management strategies are essential tools for investors seeking to protect their portfolios against potential losses and mitigate the impact of adverse market conditions. Here are some hedging techniques and risk management strategies commonly employed by investors:

1. Diversification: Diversification involves spreading investments across different asset classes, sectors, regions, and types of securities to reduce portfolio risk. By diversifying, investors can lower the correlation between assets and minimize the impact of adverse events affecting any single investment.

2. Options Contracts: Options contracts provide investors with the right, but not the obligation, to buy or sell an asset at a predetermined price (strike price) within a specified time frame. Put options can be used to hedge against a decline in the value of a security or index, while call options can hedge against a rise in prices. Options can also be used to generate income through covered call writing or protect gains through protective puts.

3. Futures Contracts: Futures contracts allow investors to hedge against price fluctuations in commodities, currencies, interest rates, and stock indices. By entering into futures contracts, investors can lock in prices for future delivery, protecting against adverse price movements.

4. Short Selling: Short selling involves selling borrowed securities with the expectation that their price will decline, allowing the investor to buy them back at a lower price and profit from the difference. Short selling can be used as a speculative strategy or as a hedge against long positions in related securities.

5. Inverse ETFs: Inverse exchange-traded funds (ETFs) are designed to deliver the opposite returns of a particular index or asset class. These ETFs can be used to hedge against declines in specific sectors or markets, providing inverse exposure to underlying securities.

6. Stop Loss Orders: Stop loss orders are instructions to sell a security once it reaches a predetermined price level,

limiting potential losses. Stop-loss orders help investors manage risk by automatically triggering a sale when prices fall below a certain threshold, preventing further losses in the event of a market downturn.

7. Asset Allocation Rebalancing: Regularly rebalancing asset allocations ensures that investment portfolios remain aligned with investors' risk tolerance and investment objectives. By periodically reallocating assets to maintain target allocations, investors can reduce portfolio risk and capture potential gains from market fluctuations.

8. Dynamic Hedging Strategies: Dynamic hedging strategies involve actively adjusting portfolio exposures based on changing market conditions and risk

factors. These strategies use quantitative models, technical analysis, and macroeconomic indicators to identify and capitalize on market trends while managing downside risk.

It's important for investors to carefully assess the costs, risks, and potential benefits of hedging techniques and risk management strategies before implementing them. Additionally, consulting with a financial advisor or investment professional can provide personalized guidance tailored to individual investment goals and risk profiles.

- Government Policies and Inflation Control Mechanisms

Government policies play a crucial role in controlling inflation and maintaining economic stability. Various mechanisms and tools are employed by governments and central banks to manage inflation effectively. Here are some key government policies and inflation control mechanisms:

1. Monetary Policy: Central banks, such as the Federal Reserve in the United States, use monetary policy tools to control inflation. One primary tool is the adjustment of interest rates. By raising interest rates, central banks can reduce the money supply, curb borrowing and spending, and dampen inflationary pressures. Conversely, lowering interest

rates stimulates economic activity and inflation during periods of low growth or deflationary pressures.

2. Open Market Operations: Central banks conduct open market operations to buy or sell government securities in the open market. By purchasing government bonds, central banks inject liquidity into the financial system, stimulating lending and economic activity. Conversely, selling bonds reduces liquidity, tightening monetary conditions, and curbing inflationary pressures.

3. Reserve Requirements: Central banks mandate reserve requirements for commercial banks, specifying the proportion of deposits that banks must hold as reserves. By adjusting reserve requirements, central banks can influence

the amount of money banks can lend, thereby affecting overall money supply growth and inflationary pressures.

4. Quantitative Easing (QE): During periods of economic downturn or deflationary pressures, central banks may implement quantitative easing programs. QE involves the purchase of long-term securities, such as government bonds and mortgage-backed securities, to inject liquidity into the economy and lower long-term interest rates. QE aims to stimulate borrowing, investment, and spending, thereby boosting inflation and supporting economic recovery.

5. Fiscal Policy: Governments can implement fiscal policy measures to influence inflationary pressures. Expansionary fiscal policies, such as

increased government spending or tax cuts, can stimulate aggregate demand and inflation. Conversely, contractionary fiscal policies, such as spending cuts or tax hikes, can dampen inflationary pressures by reducing aggregate demand.

6. Wage and Price Controls: In extreme cases of hyperinflation or runaway inflation, governments may implement wage and price controls to limit the increase in wages and prices. While these measures can provide temporary relief from inflationary pressures, they often distort market mechanisms, leading to supply shortages, black markets, and economic inefficiencies.

7. Inflation Targeting: Many central banks adopt inflation targeting frameworks, setting explicit inflation targets and

adjusting monetary policy to achieve them. Inflation targeting enhances transparency, accountability, and credibility of central bank actions, anchoring inflation expectations and promoting price stability over the medium term.

8. Exchange Rate Policy: Governments may use exchange rate policies to manage inflationary pressures, particularly in open economies with flexible exchange rates. Appreciating or depreciating the domestic currency can affect import prices, influencing overall inflation levels.

Overall, effective inflation control requires a coordinated approach combining monetary, fiscal, and regulatory policies to achieve price stability and sustainable economic growth. Central banks and governments must carefully balance competing objectives, such as controlling inflation, promoting employment, and fostering financial stability, to ensure macroeconomic stability and well-being for citizens.

www.ingramcontent.com/pod-product-compliance
Lightning Source LLC
Chambersburg PA
CBHW071101290526
45795CB00004B/1597